For Ellen:

... in friendship,
joy,
hope &
love, ...

Joshua

Evening Palette

a poetry collection

by

Jo Lee Dibert-Fitko

Copyright © 2002 by Jo Lee Dibert-Fitko

ISBN 0-7414-1231-4

Published by:

PUBLISHING.COM

519 West Lancaster Avenue
Haverford, PA 19041-1413
Info@buybooksontheweb.com
www.buybooksontheweb.com
Toll-free (877) BUY BOOK
Local Phone (610) 520-2500
Fax (610) 519-0261

Printed in the United States of America

Printed on Recycled Paper

Published September, 2002

There are no days in life so
memorable as those which
vibrated to some stroke of the
imagination.

Ralph Waldo Emerson (1803-1882)

CONTENTS

Primary Moves

Vibrant colors
of
primary splashed sails.
Bouncing triangles
to
squinting eye views
when
waters potent
quickly slice and sink,
slap against boundaries
and
microphone soft sounds.
Molded vessels
pierce
an afternoon sky,
following the cadence
of
wind and waves.
Proceeding across
the dance floor blue
with
the slickest
and sweetest
of
primary moves.

Saturday Bread

We stood in line on the sidewalk
out front.
Spindly eight year old legs
fingering coins in the deep pockets
of our jackets.
Breathing quicker.
Inhaling deeper the intoxication
of Saturday morning Irish bread.
O'Kelly's Bakery
feeding the people parade
this soft,
fresh,
warm affection.
We stuck our noses in
the brown crunchy sack
all the way home.
Picking at the crust
for teasing crumbs.
Sitting eagerly round the
kitchen oak table.
Gold trimmed plates.
Creamy butter.
Small jar of cherry preserves.
Quietly satiating a desire created
and satisfied by
a
simple, plain white loaf.

(memories circa 1963/Flint, MI)

Opening Day

It was the only day
when skipping school was okay.
Almost ordained.
Teachers envied our planned escape.
Tuning in on radios.
Sparse minutes between classes to
catch the score.
Friends begging for brought home tokens.
A felt monogrammed pennant.
Glossy photos' program book.
The few peanuts left in a
crunchy white bag.
They couldn't be there with you.
Climbing steep cement ramps.
Meeting sunshine drenched bleachers.
Saying hello to flags dancing atop centerfield
walls .
Bags on the lines. Plumped and ready for spike's
first attack. Colorful maze of eager fans.
Vendors shouting.
Advertisers boasting spirits renewed.
Excitement grabbed the broad steel posts,
plopping itself in flip down seats.
Michigan and Trumbull scooped up baseball.
Dished it out in this stadium proud.
Skipping school on opening day was
scribbling yourself into baseball history.
Memories painted with catches and runs.
Torn out newspaper pages taped to bedroom
walls. Mailing to yourself again and again the
first picture postcard of spring.

Memories of Tiger Stadium/ Detroit, MI.

Latex White

Pry open eagerly
the
lidded gallon
because
there is something
about
  white paint.
A massive vanilla
malt
that sucks up
through the straw
to
throat's downhill
  slide
and stick stirring
contents
like a huge vat
  encourage me
to dive in for
a porcelain dressing
of slick,
  shiny clean
drippings,
then sponge myself
against
your porous canvas
begging.
This stark bold
contrast to everything
  teases
primary's colors to
bright displays

and
a two- coat milkiness
denies mockingly
   you ever
existed.
Creamery richness.
Luscious diversion.
   I'd like to
dip my toes in
your tub
and stamp an all day
   walking trail
   of ivory
spontaneity,
then savor the
pearly tipped bristles
   and slink
   away for
graffiti's glowing
   runaway
      finale.

Morning Green

For
the first time
this year,
morning's
yanked away drapes
displayed
a carpeted lawn.
Overnight
she had sucked up
moon's density.
Stole slyly
golden sun's strength.
Spreading
long and lush
a new green breakfast.
Flaunting
healthy freshness.
Asking bare feet
in teasing silence
to
simply come out
and
play.

Alter Ego

Nosy feline.
Not that anyone else ever
   calls you that.
No,
   they call you
   Sweetie,
   Mister Purr
   and
   Almost Human.
You make your rounds through
this condo look-alike community.
Furry face pressed up against
   patio windows.
Muddy paw prints across
   freshly washed decks.

They deny
   giving you treats and
   letting you inside
but
   your body arrives home
   room temperature warm on the
   coldest of days.
I see that smirk across your face
when you curl up on the rug.
That brain of yours filled with
   what you saw and heard.
   Gossip. Rumors. Not so idle talk.
Tabloid reporter with
   paparazzo eyes
parading the neighborhood as
a gray and white tabby.

For Gene Kelly

Do you remember what you did to me
   when I first saw you?
   You they labeled the "song and dance man."
   It was a Sunday and you didn't know
     I was a newcomer to your talent.
The smile in your eyes was intended just for me.
It was reflecting my own as I felt the music within.
   Your body- suave, elegant, moving in a style
   possessive of you.
   A sensuality of dance, form and energy.
You grabbed me and took me swaying, flying in
   unrepeated patterns.
I could feel the strength, electricity in your muscles,
   beckoning me on,
   though I sat glued in front of the television,
   mesmerized by your being.
Beyond infatuation and thrills
   as you fed me with hopes and dreams
   that I, too, could be a model of performance.
The tunes – light, melodic, swimming through me.
I stared at my feet and legs.
New appendages I had yet to experience.
The rhythm of notes pulsating through my throat.

How many years ago was that?

The script not dated by years that have passed.
Music and dance surviving a futile comparison to
   your modern brothers.
Let me cut you out of your celluloid strip,
keep you alive in your form and grace.

We've danced through the living room so many
times, my arms folded around a piece of air.
Your surrogate.
I've taken my umbrella and paraded through
puddles, singing the lyrics, happy in the
reminiscing, splashing the wetness to let me
know
you are there.
    Your body has aged.
    The spontaneity of 1952 folded neatly.
    Tucked away in a khaki pocket of your closet.
    The soles on your shoes worn from making love
    to so many dance floors.
You continue feeding me a memory of
enthusiasm.
    Unquenched emotions.
    A content feeling of displacement within the era
        of movie musicals.
The era is not lost.
My affection and esteem for you survive.
The wetness cascading my face as I pounce
    through the puddles
    never felt
        so good.

Lake Superior Performance

Where did you come from?
Waves building up for miles
   have filled the stage
   like a chorus line.
Rhythm movements,
streamlined in unison
   come crashing against
   an audience.
The sandy shore in applause
soaked up your being.
   White fluffiness
   exploding foam at your
   finale.

Are you always stealing the show?
In envious helplessness
   I accept your performance,
   challenging not the beauty
   of the powerful.
We decorate ourselves in
costumes grandiose.
   Glitter. Lighting of a spectrum.
   Makeup to enhance. Accentuate.
While you in your simplicity
are so complex.
   So fascinating.
   Who could upstage you?

Better we as the cast
   take a seat in your theater.
   Merely absorb the sight of your gift.
Drench us in wetness refreshing.
   Encore me until my senses
   are exhausted.

Crayola® Closet

Oh
to be a wardrobe of
Crayola® Markers
so I might colorize myself
in pastel, bold and fluorescent
saturations.
Occasional basic primaries and
points of reference more like
splotches that linger beyond paper.
Company kept with unusual
shapes spawn creativity.
Colors that visually melt and massage
invite fingered touches.
Hot magenta lends infinite hues.
Neon yellow sizzles the edges.
Goldenrod, orchid, forest green
satisfy nature's stage.
Midnight blue asks for anything
but sleep.
Raspberry, lime, peach,
sherbet themselves in cones
that drip.
The canvas white parades
like brazen Broadway.
Glowing pinwheels spark breezes.
Mellow tints smoothly soothe.
Exhausted rainbows,
snuggled into caps,
tuck themselves into neat restful
boxes and choose at whim or
plotted deviance
the colors of choreography.

Grape Jam

Early autumn day.
Sweat dripping with tears streaks blush
down my cheeks like finger paint .
Sweatshirt chilled dampness.
Brown working gloves tear,
saw at grapevine's tangled grip.
Yanking stubbornness from fence's wire
where massive branches hang heavy with fruit.
Odd couple.
This knotted bark refusing to yield it's brittleness
while ripeness slightly fingered parades to the
ground in release. They were your vines,
your plantings now pruned and invaded by
my prying shears.
This year's naked pantry spaces will recall
last year's small glass jars. Paraffin sealed.
Luscious grape jam. Scooped up in spoonfuls.
Dripping down chins or the sides of
buttermilk biscuits.
In tiredness I plop to the ground.
Exhausted. Knowing this deep entanglement
will produce life sprouting again.
Promising more bundles of purple sweetness.
But for now it's too soon.
The pain of losing you still fresh. Tender.
So with work gloves discarded,
finger slowly extended,
I close my eyes, trace this future season of
perpetuation and simply lick my lips with
the taste of a memory.

Poetry Buffet

I have covered my table
with the delicacy of fine woven linen.
Polished silver's shining enunciations.
You arrive with butter dripping words,
warm French bread whose crusty shell
collapses to soft center's eagerness.

Tender crumbs playfully licked
reveal porcelain smooth speech.
Tease hunger's mounting appetite.
Tangy juices released from your
lingual fruits are sweet desserts.
Secretive trespassers.

I scoop you up in emotion's frosting.
Spread you delectably thin
or gushing whipped thickness.
Confection samplers of savory verse
promise always a ripened abundance.

Just buffet me.
Quench the thirsty cup.
Drip seductively that rich mellowing
cream of language.
Entice me.
I'll be the spoon arousing slowly,
waltzing gently through your
dark strong coffee
    waiting.

Mrs. Irving

When I was six,
she lived down the street,
on the corner,
in the old white house
with forest green trim.
The oldest house on the block.
Even older than Mrs. Irving herself
whose thick beige socks sagged
under thin cotton dresses.
Pressed linen aprons skimmed
her heavy black shoes.

She was from England.
I liked her voice,
the way her words sounded
settling around the carved
piano legs or resting on lace
doilies of overstuffed chairs.
Her creamy skin spotlessly scrubbed,
fresh on hot afternoons when
she baked oatmeal cookies,
piled high on china plates
beside dripping cold glasses
of home-delivered milk.

Once a week during summer breaks,
I picked dandelion bouquets
from the Smith's backyard,
tied them with shiny ribbons,
slipped them into fresh water vases
on Mrs. Irving's big oak table.
She told me she loved my dandelions.

Called them God's favorite flower.
Said that's why He planted
so many of them,
why they grew so fast and took on
sun's golden glow.
The yellow petals matched her
apron strings,
the trim around her cookie plates,
the rich blond light from her
brass piano lamp.

She let me play that piano,
plunking unknown keys,
singing invented words,
making lyrics rhyme while
her thin wrinkled fingers
knitted fast and exact
slippers for season's change.
On January mornings,
that thick wool would feel soft
and warm across cold linoleum floors.
Skeins of yellow shades would
colorize my feet, lace up high over
bony ankles like oversized baby booties.

When Mrs. Irving died,
I wore those slippers to the corner,
scattered dandelions across her porch.
A man in black swept them away,
after the funeral, but not before
they were trampled over.
Yellow petals grinding into pitted steps.
Milky stains soaking coarse cement.
Smashed stems scattering a manicured lawn.

In time,
Someone with a different name moved in.
Neighborhoods change. Yellow aluminum siding
replaced the old white paint.
Talk spread quickly over backyard fences.
   Who would choose such a color?
      Mrs. Parker wanted to know.
      Mr. Garland called it disgusting.
      Mrs. Larsen said it really stuck out.
      Made that old corner house just not fit in.

But I liked it.
I liked it a lot.
Tasting once again Mrs. Irving's oatmeal cookies,
hearing the musical words of her
kitchen voice.
Watching skinny hands move with
creative play.
That summer,
the dandelions from Smith's backyard
grew extra tall and very strong,
spreading a thick vibrant yellow carpet,
dancing freely with afternoon breezes
and
I never picked even one.

The Dog From Three Blocks Over

He or she startled me.
I jumped with the wet licks
behind my knees.
Milky Lab.
    Don't follow me.
You became my walking partner.
Catch-up companion.
Escorting me home.
No collar. No ID.
Slopping up water from a green bowl
retrieved from my kitchen sink.
    I don't have time to play.
Cottage cheese carton lids
as makeshift Frisbees®.
A round of fetch with
broken up sticks.
Last year's tennis ball
now sticky with drool.
    Okay. Enough. Go home now.
You curl up on the outdoor mat.
Afternoon's welcome nap.
Autumn's sun makes your coat
bristly warm to the touch.
    I mean it. You can't stay here.
Belly rising over slow easy breathing.
Lids closed over fudge brown eyes.
Tail thumping in metronome pace.
My lunch on a plate by your side.

Flavigny-sur-Ozerain

Silence fusing harmony in this
narrow medieval hamlet.
Cobblestone streets. Smooth slate.
Aging terracotta. Flower boxes boasting
vibrant palettes against home fronts
of soft gray. Warm creamery hues.
Deep moist shade of hidden recesses.
Gardens ripening to sun's watch.

Faces donating "bon jour" smiles
gently place me centuries past while
in the moment inspiring.
I hear my breathing.
Feel my heart pulsing.
Feet pacing with expectation.
Fortress stonewalls keep out. Hold in.
Circumference me with a hug.

Settling into café seating,
my fingers fumble through this
French dictionary.
Searching for words that define.
Closing the cover in satisfied futility.
Wine glasses held up to filtering sun.
Deep blood red. But of course.
This village is kin to life.
Savoring senses. Sipping it slowly.
Drop by drop.
Waiting. Wondering
While my thoughts flirt quietly
with her history.

January Effect

They call it
the lake effect.
Huge bonded waters.
Impacting strength winds.
Decisions handed down from
boardroom skies regard
no property private.
Slapping steep mountains white
against flatness of homes.
Between tall trees,
stretching long snow hammocks.

Fast roads driven like
worn stale habits become
hide and seek excursions.
Tense necks. Gripping hands.
Vacillating language to
cope or create.
Claiming it drives us away
to mild southern winters.
But
for most of us,
it keeps us here.
Boots sink deeper.
Shovels guard frozen doors.
Wild vanilla displays
drape thickly,
slowly
down the January
of our years.

Planted Farmers

It's that time of day
when you're caught between
humid dusk and a smudging
drooping nightfall.
Out on this Illinois highway
where the corn grows
thick and long for
miles and hours.
Silos protrude like perpendicular
rockets to defy you claiming
everything as flat.

Farmhouses planted on
acres apart make you question
if they know their neighbors,
if it even matters,
or if nights like this find them
on sunken sofas, worn from
sunlight's pounding heat and
endless soil's stubbornness.
You wonder if numbed
conversations must suffice
and weak hugs through
sweaty stained shirts offer
encouragement enough.

I'm a passenger on this highway,
keeping time with the tire's
monotony, counting the tiered
utility poles, the faded
leaning signs and the bugs
our headlights absorb.
But I can't count the corn,
those lined up stately rows.

Capacious piled up miles
slowly filling into hanging
calendar years.

Sticking my head out a
rolled down window,
air cooled teasing of pent up
rain strokes my cheek.
Wet answers to streak
parched faces and dry,
cracking land.
Knowing only then,
after dried up days and
weakening selfish droughts,
the hugs of planted farmers
on screened porches waiting
must be longer and stronger
and deeper than I thought.

Celebrating George
(George Sand/1804-1876)

The camaraderie struck me.
I saw her riding fearlessly
on horseback. Hair flying.
Facing the briskness of the wind.
Clad in men's coat and slacks.
I could hear Baroness Dudevant
mock the speaker. Telling me the ride
can be rough at times. Persistence
such an unglamorous trait.

Passionate writer.
Spewing papered words of magnificence.
Confessional of political frustrations.
Social mores. The public debated whether
your attire or novels or morals were
more shocking or scandalous.
As if the sensitivity of a woman's truth
must always lie in delicate innocence,
harbored guilt or the softness of skin.
You produced genuine life on paper.
Adjectives stark with no regrets
and they squirmed.

I know you in the present tense.
Feel driven by the gutsy emotionalism
of your language. I imagine us in
soft red velvet gowns, exchanging names,
reciting our wares in the sweetest of
voices. Judgments still the same.
Laughing. Crying. Screaming. Rejoicing.
Writing fiction to tease the facts.
Pens dripping honest ink. Horses
unbridled for a zealous ride.

Evening Palette

I don't sink
   into the blues
     at sunset,
but sometimes a
   dash of screeching pink,
     fuzzy peach or
       drifting lavender.
I let them
   have their way.
     Changing hues.
Spreading around like
   paint swatches freed
     from their racks.
Penetrating sky walls
   while elusively haunting.
     Donning new nightly
costumes in silky sleekness
   and soft flannel.
     Flaunting scripts
totally unrehearsed.
   Dropping hints that
     the real show begins
behind black velvet curtains
   after they've shut off
     my view,
Leaving me quite comfortably
   incomplete in a
     vacated theater
with a bare palette begging
  and brushes eager to
    dip
      and
        dance.

Breakfast

This morning
black birds
crowd each other
out
for the few pieces
of stale and
crusty bread.
Semblance like
a spreading pile
of dark thick tar
across fresh green
summer grass.
Their hungry
pitch strained screeches
smother the air
then succumb to a
muted drone.
Searching beaks
clean the
ground laid table
with one
picked up swoop.
Departing as promptly
as they arrived.
I'm left staring
with an empty
plastic bag dangling.
My guests' gratuity
paving the sky
for a hundred runway's
crisscross view.

Only On a Winter's Night

The sky-
　　gentle gray matte' of city outer limits
　　appears as ashes still warm and soft.
　　Fluffed up pillows hanging from above.
Constant observers,
　　protectors of white fields below.
　　Friends having never shaken hands,
　　never touching, but they have been
　　meeting each other for years.
Flood lights of city parking lots,
　　stark and brazen
　　against summer's contrasting blackness
　　are mellowed by winter's night to peachy hues,
　　　　suspending and floating,
　　　　mindless of parameters.
Boots zipped up in their heaviness are lightened,
　　become playful with mounds of feathery snow.
Quiet interrupted only by subtle gurgles
　　of sewers, seeking the clean drink that seeps
　　through their bars, quenching a thirst.
Pine trees nestled in for the evening with
　　blankets on every limb.
Smells of intoxicating newness inhaled so eagerly.
Cheeks of a pinkness painted only by winter's
　　brush and eyes given a clarity and brightness
　　by the clean damp are lost upon encountering
　　the stale heat and intruding fluorescence
　　of my home inside.
Only on a winter's night.
I peer through the curtains to absorb your
loveliness once more and
slide open the window but a crack
to preserve my freshness.

The 1968 Series

There was something about that year.
Something about that summer.
Slowly culminating in an autumn that would
explode through the static on pocket transistor
radios. An afternoon science class abandoning
the pop quizzes and experiments for black and
white TV.

Gathered round the teacher's desk.
We huddled as one in nervous anxiety.
Muffling our excitement.
Clenching our fists so tightly.
The skinny legs on those pedestal stools
rocked and ground into the creaking floor
till you couldn't hold the screams and the cheers.

Tight third floor windows were pushed up wildly
to let loose the clamor down this city block and
across our own school's dusty empty benched
field. We piled on each other with jumping hugs
and
claimed blue and orange to be the best colors
in the world.
Our throats were raw after yelling.
The skin on our palms stung after so much
clapping. Eyes dripped wetness with the wonder
of that final game.

It was like a first love. Only better.
A pounding vibrancy in our hearts that left nerves
dancing. We all wore Old English "D's" on pretend
jerseys and swung bats with fierce grips that
clenched our entire bodies.

At thirteen I heard the Tigers really roar.
I saw them pluck the feathers from those St.
Louis birds. They brought home the pennant.
Embraced the glory of World Series Champs and
dug their claws into my memory.
Right down to the roots
which each spring sprout and spread
a ball diamond's green- grassed freshness.
The eager hopes of a new season at bat.

Celebrating the Detroit Tigers/
Memories from Longfellow Junior High School:
Flint, MI

The Loss/Part One

Anxious
  for the ache
  from his death,
  choking grip
  on my muscles,
  individualizing
  my nerves
to overwhelm me.
Longed for moment
of immobility.
  The saturation point
  rocky and tipsy.
Roller coaster emotions
bounce me with a thud.
  Diffuse my thoughts.
  Diffuse me just this once.
Make me incapable of analysis,
the backup of questions,
or memories.
Searching labels for this
new and gutted feeling
  not defined by any
  other event,
  by any other person.
Cringing coolly at the
unknown. Weeping pulls me
into a puddle. Drying to a void.
Pain so intense.
  Part of me has been
  yanked away.
Apprehension. Reaching out.
  Fingering the open wounds
  where the gentlest of touches
  screeches of sadness.

A Concert Tuxedo

Down the narrow bumpy brick street
she drove slowly on those humid summer nights,
kids piled in a back seat station wagon,
our necks craned out windows,
inhaling in gulps the aroma of fresh baking bread.
Those were Mondays. Late. Following the concerts
in downtown Willson Park where our shirts stuck
creased to our skin and we took off shoe's
confinement to keep tempo with
the grass and the Motor City Concert Band.
Music that seeped dancing out of conformist
limbs. Guttural humming from an audience
indulged. Yet we seemed so bland compared to
the conductor in his crisp white tuxedo and
ebony bow tie. Frank Tambourino. A destined
name. I imagined him at rehearsals. Rolled up
cotton sleeves. Angular arms flying. Musically
exploiting all the percussion instruments. It was
easy to draw such fantasies when the music
slowed and softened, quenching adult requests
for hand holding melodies while sedating small
children sprawled out on worn wool blankets,
tummies heavy with intermission's popcorn and
syrupy orangeade. On those nights the bread rose
with the yeast of Broadway tunes. I dreamed of
abandoning my flute for a flamboyant trombone,
stretching the sliding, flashy metal, basking in the
beat of the musical encore, knowing on one
lucent summer stage, a white tuxedo sure felt
good.

Memories circa 1965/Flint, MI

Crystal Respite

Some things are
slipped into easily.
Smoothly.
Gentle currents over
sandy bottoms.
Singular canoe sliding
through Crystal River's
opening.
Down the aisle,
parting silky green
blades and curious fish.
Past herons perched
on wildflower shores.
Lily pads as
water hammocks.
Ebony winged dragonflies,
emerald torsos glowing,
scope our pale skin,
tour us by
twisted fallen trees
posed as gallery
sculptures.
Breezes fresh
comb our hair,
sift through our
clothes,
follow us home
to potpourri rooms
with
sweet lingering scents
of cedar and
somewhere else.

West Virginia Interstate 77

Rocky. Scrubbed.
Cool. Warm gray.
Teasing highway's edge
with slate's jagged
fermentation.
Swaying road to passage
stepped platforms.
Carpeted trees of .
broccoli tipped heights
befriend small
whitewashed dwellings of
pocketed towns.
You monopolize my view
with wide angled
pleasure like
thousands of lush green
arms who ascend
and descend me.
Teal hazed footings
squint at a distance.
Steel beams of
forest emeralds
bridge long over
deep river veins.
Sun bronzed hues
collapse with day's
finale
until mountain hugs
gradually release me
to photograph once again
morning's new
postcards.

Tuesday

September is one of my
favorite months.
Summer's finale flirting subtly
with the beginning of autumn's
dancing colors.
Temperatures mild.
Children back to school.
Expectant changes welcomed.
A wedding anniversary celebrated.

This year's anniversary
brought more.
Life dangling in thick choking air.
Metaphors stretched to the max.
Replays that glazed our eyes.
We screamed in horror.
We wept.
We prayed.
Adrenalin activated.
Exhaustion covering.
Peripheral nerves snipped right off,
searing pain with no place to go.

It took two weeks for me to grasp
my writing pen again,
perched in my Chevy truck
bound for the Saginaw YMCA.
Listening to The Best of Simon and Garfunkel,
"The Only Living Boy in New York".
I pulled over into the Sunoco gas station.
Scrounged the back seat
madly for a remnant of paper
on which to write.

The back of a 7-Eleven receipt
dated September 11th,
reminding us to "Have A Nice Day".

Pen in hand.
Movement stops.
Emotions churn,
desperate for graphic expression.
I shove the pen back in my purse.
Close my eyes.
Calm myself into slower breathing.

It's not the uncertainty of
which words to use nor
the length of title to employ.
But it seems,
in this moment,
thousands of definitions in the
thickest of dictionaries
have slipped off their pages
into one futile pile.
Lame.

...with hope

Internal Page

Often
it seems
when I withdraw to
meet quietness,
I could linger for hours.
Embracing necessity.
Fueling printed words.
  Always have.
Since childhood afternoons.
Stretched out on backyard blankets.
Wiggling toes across woven cotton.
Library books piled.
Squinted stares at clouds'
patterned language.
Pen. Paper.
Pillowed theme book pages
whose welcomed respite
became my own.
  Then
  as now
calmly sculpting
mind's collection.
Deep blue ink
spawning trails.
Giving an alphabet
  her voice.

In memory of Paul W. Wightman
Ninth Grade English Teacher, Mentor/Friend

Eglise
(Saint Antoine Church/Bar-le-Duc, France)

Antiquity. Stone and mortar.
Pillars. Statues of carved expletion.
Paintings descriptive. Faces lit softly from behind.
Luminescent skin. Silky cloth.
Visions of saints scrolling the lengthy halls.
My eyes circumference this eglise.
Placing myself at an altar, then upon a wicker chair.
One wooden leg scrapes against ancient tile.
Deep echoes. Awakening history at rest.
Spirituality floats. Sneaks up through crevices.
Leans into tenth century walls.
Sits in my lap quietly. Nervously.
To feel at once surrounded. Abandoned.
Joy and anger punching it out in futility.
Thrilled by structural beauty yet vexed by truths exposed in collection baskets rich. Prayers of revenge. Confessionals thick with deposited guilt.
Religion may free some while dissecting others.
One peeling strand at a time. Beliefs parading around in suits of war. Savoring fullness when ripe with glory. Crying in despair with deaths of defeat.
Incongruity of thoughts. Repetition of action.
Professing what? To whom? Christianity overflowing with love yet in the name of it, human horrors.
Sects pitted against each other. My ancestors,
like millions preceding could only claim life by
fleeing with it. Ten centuries later these walls are
still damp to the touch. Seeping. Staining.
Pleading. They probably always will be.
Tears are like that you know.

Fracture

Gray sky on this
March Sunday oppresses
like the heavy droopiness
of November.
Stuck between seasons
of indecision.
Future's plotting anxious
yet fringed with the irritating
scrape of debris.
Dragging it's feet with
no place to cling.

One mundane highway
absorbs constant the tread
of worn miles,
tired eyes and limp soul.
Not quite classified,
this to or from
yet slapped with orange
fluorescent reminders.
Barricades of the bumps and
crevices of sharp angles.

Blockaded fresh soul
harnessed for hot tar's
suffocation.
The breathing intensity
of one mind smoldering.
Searing edges to seal or expose.
Fractured me.
Knowing and not knowing.
Gray is but
a neutral color.

Playful

Shuffling fantasies
probe.
Wind.
Loose yarn defying
knitted form.
Cryptic smiles.
Whispers incognito
meet their match.
Drop deeply into
voiceless words.
Mindless.
Mindful.
Playfully merging.
Something
effervescent
tingles.

Claysburg

Grassy stain of morning's dew.
Sunk within this Pennsylvania mountain.
Revisiting the ache. Rejoining the comfort.
Flipped sides of pleasantry and loss.
That ancient house whose wood raw thirsts for
a coat of whiteness yet remains pacified
with the ease of bareness.

As the fog lifts, there's the assurance
of it's return. Stained colors of life
with wash and wear tags can't remove
these scrapings of a season.
One suitcase dragged from here to there.
Overstuffed. Tugged zippered closure whose
contents promise, at some point... lightness.

Reception

Hear the canvas melody.
Stanzas of rhythm wind.
This white sailed dream
floats round and through
and within.
Comfortable golden sun
clothing tinged by the aquamarine
splashed wetness.
Sliding currents yield to wood's
glowing massive sculpture.
Fresh spontaneous dance,
gulping scents of nature's
soothing holiday.
Serve it up with tempting blue
waves and the rich syrup of a
melting sky.
Savor the spirited dream until
the promising voyage renders
again and again an endless
welcoming reception.

For my husband, Captain Gary Fitko

Sour Milk

Forty-seven years of marriage.
They know enough to go on Thursdays.
In the morning. Avoiding the
congestion of Saturdays. Whining
children dragged along with empty
stomachs. She halts in front of the
peanut butter. Asks about his favorite
brand. He shrugs his shoulders with an
I don't care or I don't know response.
Shuffling past the lettuce heads.
Rummaging through. Thinking everything
shrinks with age. Routine egg carton checks
for the cracked and gooey ones.
Slide them to the back. Next to the butter
surrogates with clever names and bland
plastic tastes. Pushing through to the cereal
aisle full of commercials' battles. A hand
clenched with coupons stuffs them back in
her purse as oatmeal's familiarity wins. Boxes
piled, smashed, protruding from overstocked
shelves. They squint at printed ingredients he
can't pronounce and she doesn't want to meet.
Just return to the produce where food can be
recognized. Squeezing and smelling still
somewhat acceptable. Tastes you can predict.
But the cantaloupe is spongy. The vegetables are
losing the struggle to remain firm and green. So
the few groceries huddle tightly in the huge cart.
Grab a can of beans, tomato soup and a slippery
carton of milk. It tasted better when home
delivered and housed in glass. And the meat. He
remembers the wrapped up contents in crisp
white paper. I don't like all the Styrofoam® he

grunts. She kicks in motion one disoriented wheel while conforming to the checkout lane. He recalls the bag boy's face. Freckled with crooked glasses. Always laughing. His wife awkwardly smiles. Johnny retired thirty years ago when the store closed at eight or nine or something like that. The sparse groceries in this bag seem so heavy. So heavy. The milk will sour before we ever get it home...

Dancing Advent

Just yesterday
this room was swollen
with air stale
and insipid
        like winter's
used up months.
The planted life
        with roots aching
had hibernated in this
        cracking lame dirt
for too many smothered days.
But this morning,
window's lazy yawn
        was challenged with
a dose of seasoned change,
        like scrambling
dancers late for rehearsal,
rushing in, perking up
the wilted green until the
inhaled tonic was
        almost musical,
then slowly letting go
with escaping metered sighs.
Soft presumptive hopes
of a long running stage
        booked by
this performance ingested.
Ushered in by stems
        stretching quizzically.
Meeting sunlight's arms.
Wishing to be yanked away with
a propensity to the
melting advent of spring.

Cabin Full Moon

A cue ball
escaped beyond
earth's
tangible reach.
Huge white
globe,
smeared with
gray landscaped
wanderings,
dotted ivory
craters.
Night clouds of
soft striated
cotton mesh
cushion me,
weave their way
through the
spreading
navy pulp.

The view fills
deeply
yet with morning's
creeping entrance,
clarity of
nightscapes,
imagery evoked,
will disappear.
Only with eyes
closed can
pictures rekindle.
A flooding
effervescence to
satiate the day.

Wearing Pearls

You ought to be wearing pearls
        he said
as the syrupy sweetness poured
down me, coating me with a glaze.
The stickiness clung to soles.
Knowing it would slow my movement.
Mark the trail of my direction.

      It's a path
you'll never follow. Safer not getting
stuck in the tackiness. Sure. I ought to be
wearing pearls all right, so I may glisten
through the night in round smooth
shapes that would comfort you,
though to me they lie heavy on my neck.

      You chose
the beads, so exact in size, so predictable
to view. Strung in a regiment of orderly
fashion. To your satisfaction, circles
don't define a beginning or an end.

      I wore
those pearls, awkwardly struggling to
undo the clasp you skillfully joined,
until finally the roundness became distorted,
splattering into sharp pieces of omniscience.
Your stare now failed to define their existence.

      Failed to define me.
The choking had made me gasp for air.
I found you stroking for the last time the
soft jewels around my neck.

      I pulled
on the string. The fragility for once
pleased me. It broke with the tug, marbles
fleeing and bouncing in all directions.
An uncontrollable collection of a necklace
never to be recovered.

      Your glare
held a fearful surprise and I felt nothing.
You frowned and I responded with a smile,
kicking away those stones left in my path.
I rewound the tape to its point of origin.

      You ought
   to be wearing pearls
      I said.

Feast of Thanks

We begin the feast.
Colors, smells,
tastes of livestock.
Harvested display.
Planted life
rewinds its' journey.
Embryonic seeds sewn
thick beneath
earth's tablecloth.
Seeking,
sought by
sun and rain,
farmers' endless toil.
Their union sprouting
sustenance on our plates,
nurturance to our souls.
Reminding all
this bounty set before us
is one prayer richly
answered
and another yet
begun.

Deep Hovering Blue

You've got a stare
that inches up and
down me with a
massive and sneaky
crawl.
I poke you here.
I sniff you there.

I'm wearing you along
this four- mile stretch
as pastel stains leak
out and over.
You affect my mood
with a quiet passion.
With an assurance
you remind of lost senses.

If I hid in recesses
you'd coax me out,
smoothing round the edges.
You bring fluorescence
out of barren drab.
Energize waning limpness.

You turn up corners
for a quirky smile,
breathing pools now
rich in bloom.
This winsome sky
so playfully unwrapping
it's
deep hovering blue.

Flip Side Ad

1934.
Her arm slid down
the side of a
shiny new Buick
until her hand grasped
the door handle.
Body poised into
perfect model molding.
Walnut hair coifed in
swimming smooth waves.
Calf length skirt
skimming warm angles
and curves.
Deep red lipstick
circling the most
inviting of smiles.
A center page spread
selling the hottest
of cars.
A sheet of advertising.
   Only it wasn't.
No female vamped here
to sell four wheeled
lines.
Not when she could
strip bright chrome
to dull bareness
in seconds.
Leave new designs
quickly outdated.
Her laughing gaze could
pierce scratches in glass.
Soft strength topple

steel to a meek limpness.
She continues masquerading
this way in family photos.
Maintaining her wit
and suave ways.
Refusing to adhere
to the pages.
It seems to me
she's always known
tactful mockery of
tasteless ads,
who really deserved
promotion's pleas
and who would crumble
into orange rust,
broken glass
and the
rotted out rubber
of decay.

In celebration of my mother, Lillian J. Dibert

Fingered Night

It was
as if
just the perception
itself
was a heated
element.
Auctioning off
glowing warmth
to but one
satisfied buyer.

Word's meltdown
lingering.
I grasp dancing air
with baton-tipped fingers.
Molding transparency
like soft clay.
Refusing to stagnate
in form or voice.

I like this
conglomerate adrift.
Pick and choose
pictures.
Loosened imagination.
Night settles on
tipsy fringes of
teasing possibilities.
Lyrics tenderly
abandoned
blush.

Caribbean Discovery/
British Virgin Islands

Scorching fire
  of this
    equator clutched sun
permeates my raw
  northern skin
until
    turquoise blue
tempts me into
cooling ocean baths.

Luminous purples,
sleek silvers
  dress underwater performers.
Rich history speaks in
  dark virgin faces,
  billowing sails,
    tropical breathing music
dipped in zesty spices,
star filled nights.

There is a genius
  filling this place,
making her home in breezes
    constant,
rocking you among her
  many molded isles
    with
loosely
  fitting
    intoxication.

John and Blanche

Perhaps it was the
black and white movie in
this dark room theater
carefully recreating events
of that day.
Spliced with photos which
escaped rushing waters.
Suffocating flows.
Families decidedly posed,
delicately seated in carved
wooden frames.
Displayed proudly over
fireplace mantles.
Hauntingly odd.
Matted cardboard,
flimsy paper survived
smashing floods whose
ten- minute course broke
and entered this city.
Stealing lives.
Drowning dreams.
Fiercely gulping up property.
Anxious planned futures
spit forth in sinking mud
along devastation's path.
Explosive flames choked
dying screams.
Outstretched hands never met.
Families gutted instantly
by death.
Women widowed.
Husbands companionless.
Children at play who never
came home.

John's photographed face.
Proud successful father.
Strong loving hand resting on
Blanche's small shoulder.
Nine- year old daughter dressed
in cotton finery and lace.
Now alphabetized victims on
a museum wall.
More than a century later
crashing thunderstorms
break outside.
Deafening sounds.
Drenching sights.
A wife.
A mother
A sister
still weeping.

In memory of all victims of the Johnstown Flood
Johnstown, Pennsylvania (1889)

Human Drought

Exhausted arms
dropping a suitcase halfway
through the door.
Twelve hours late and
feeling like Hades' twin.
Finally home from
lined up cars collapsed
on expressway shoulders.
Hot metal hoods
thrown up in frustration.
Steam escaping from
sizzling radiators and
cranky drivers.
Faces pale framed stringy hair.
Hunched over backs.
Rank smells of fast food grease,
diesel fuel,
sickened our guts.
Clung to the air like
heavy starched drapes.
Bodies coated with
slimy drippings matched
scorched conversations.
Fed suffocating thoughts.
Made us forget last Wednesday.
Back porches covered
in puddles.
Flower planters overflowing.
We dashed to the car,
umbrellas overhead,
to avoid getting
drenched
by the rain.

November Photograph

Long spiny limb,
reaching out over the water
  with nothing left to
    grasp.
One leaf left,
her brown belly flickering
to erratic wind's breath.
Teetering hold by a
  singular vein.
Showing off for sun's
  spotlight.

This final tightrope
  performer.
Wide liquid net below
  who already absorbed
    the rest of her
  family.
Let them move in.
Settle down.

One flowing stream whose
  clarity will soon be muted
    by a milky freeze.
Another season. A new act.
A different set of circus
    performers.

Rough and Smooth

They're just
old baby food jars,
filled with nuts
and bolts,
screws and common
nails.
Piled up magnets.
Copper tubes.
They've slept together
for years.
Mounded thickly on
each other.
Leaning over the edges.
Hunks of chiseled Teflon®.
Large spooled wire.
Squeeze bottle lubricants
separated by
yellow sheets of advertising,
frayed cardboard boxes,
red stamped receipts.

I'm twisting off lids.
Unfolding papers.
Tracing sand paper rough
and ball bearing smoothness.
   You're still alive.
   I'm eight again.
Perched on that creaky stool.
Watching skilled hands assemble.
Letting me participate in answers.
   Twist the screwdriver.
   Tighten the vice.
   Dust off the lens.

Till the hours got so late.
Small hands couldn't prop
up my head.
Eyes drooped under waning lights.
Saturated ears could no longer listen.

Yet it was so hard to get up.
Leave.
Traipse up the stairs.
Go to bed.
There was always the possibility
I'd miss something.
   Late night discoveries.
   An experiment's finale.
Your anxious face
as
you plotted ideas.
Tonight
amid old sheet metal scraps,
dusty boxes and
stray bits of wire,
it seems
not then
but now
it turns out
I was right.

Dibert Experimental Laboratory/Flint, MI.
In memory of my father, Fred Dibert

Chicago Nights

Dreams about Chicago.
Six nights in a row.
Rushed feet on crowded walks.
Breezy lakeshore drives.
Barren old hotel rooms
with skinny hallways.
Creaky elevators that arrive
when they feel like it.
There's a focus on
thick soled shoes,
ancient carpet with
faded rose patterns,
gray slush piled
against helpless curbs.
I never see faces,
peaks of towering buildings,
light fixtures over my head.
In these nightly ventures
ethnic foods skim the surface,
noises crawl through office lobbies,
fast legs are lunch hour strangers.
This nocturnal city may decide
to move me up from the
baseboard heat, sidewalk
cracks and steaming sewers,
but then again,
fresh grass planted in
soil rich with newness
knows somebody's gonna leave
the first set of prints.
On this seventh night
in Chicago dreams,
the guts of life
begin at the bottom.

The Wait

Last year's
cornfield
pokes through
the snow.
Barn woods whimper
as winds sting
their home.
Spiny trees,
naked from
greenery's desertion
stretch angular limbs,
snap from your
stare.
Molded trails of
rusting tractors
halt at frozen fences
while
dirt mounds protrude
like mosaic kitchen
tiles.
Puffed up skies
weep
gray tinged flakes
on livestock huddled
in winter's
gluing bond.
Muted lyrics,
stored in silos
and hollow spaces,
count the days,
release their voice
in this season of wait
to the first green
blade of spring.

Mabel

After the funeral
  I tried to explain it to someone.
Someone who didn't grow up
  in the old neighborhood.
Dissecting words of a pastor
  transplanted from another city,
another congregation.
Guts unspoken were exchanged by
  the rest of us through
  clutching hugs, welled up eyes.
Faces melted and merged our pasts.
  Someone whistled over a backyard fence.
  Knocked on a screen door for two eggs.
  A roll of toilet paper.
  Borrowed the whitewall cleaner.
  Aunt Laura's frosting recipe.
  Sat in driveways on hot summer nights,
  sipping cool drinks to metronome
  sounds of feet jumping rope.
  Basketballs bouncing off homemade boards.
  We clumped together at school
  ice cream socials,
  Boy Scout meetings, voting booths or
  Vacation Bible School.

Sitting rigidly today on hard backed chairs.
  Perfectly aligned rows.
Lyrics to hymns dwindling in our throats.
Soaked tissues strangling in our palms.
Mabel's not really confined to a casket,
not when we can see her straight upright form.
Fingers planted firmly on piano keys.
Smells from Harry's cigar permeating the air.

Late dinner in large pans cooking
slowly in the oven.
We're all invited inside again.
We've seen it. Heard it. Smelled it. Tasted it
   before.
It stuck with us.
Coated our insides.
Planted warmth in our hearts.
Life's sweetness in tiny drops
   lingering on the tips
   of our eulogy tongues.

Osmosis

This music,
dreamily mystic
transforms.
Recurrent spontaneity.
Downstream.
Upstream.
Breezes faint
slide into this
post-midnight room.
Osmosis of
senses drowsy.
Sounds of such
soothing intensity
fondle me
into
weightless
evaporation.

Smells of August

Smells of August linger.
Dew hangs longer on wilting leaves.
Crickets voice their response to
frogs' deep toned verse.
Seesaw temperatures leave
grass brittle as sticks,
softened by overnight
drenching storms.

Produce makes it's way
to roadside stands,
filling us up with
crisp greenness,
tender yellows,
crunchy reds,
juicy purples.

Night walks in jauntily
this summer month,
then slows down just a bit.
Collapsing gently in
faded lawn chairs.
Exhaling over us,
one by one
the lingering smells of August.

Grand Island/North Light

The seamen of yesterday
knew her stark white edifice.
An ivory washed tower piercing
through fog and darkness.
Capturing their eyes and ears
when nighttime's blanket was
Lake Superior's cold depths.

Light welcomed as a
candle's sparked ebony.
Shoreline sounds, sights to
make the grasp of land almost
tangible.
Coveting the guide like the
longing for fresh memories.

Loved ones planted on summer porches.
Shawls for warmth when hugs must wait.
Eeriness of a Great Lake nocturnal.
Fueling minds with possibilities.
Tales retold to satiate the hours,
mingling with the seamen's love
of the fierce gulping blue.

Evening's long crashing storms
shower electrical movements that shudder,
shrieking of power as ships shiver
in response.
Pelting waves in arrogant defiance
finally collapse from interminable nights.
Intensity is slowly tamed.
Mellow murmurs now soothe the deck.
Slivers of sunshine breakfast the morn.

Jutting lands unscathed lighthouse
erupting through massive rocks jagged
remains stability's grip to shore.
Keepers of the Light, weary, sleepless,
dutiful to the tasks at hand.
Performance hours edged with expectation.
Their leadership a respite to cradle
both ship and crew,
who breathe constant with faces relieved
their deep subtle thanks.

For Edward S. Morrison (1878-1908)
Great Uncle/Assistant Lighthouse Keeper

Cat Sabbatical

Lately
he's been climbing on the dressers
and not so stable shelves,
pawing the paintings and photos,
tipping the view to a crooked display.
He's been squirming his agile body
onto the bookcase, squeezing in behind
the top row, knocking over discriminately
Balzac, Hellman, an extinct Merck Manual.
He's been sleeping in the bathroom sink,
disposing of liquid soap containers,
vainly staring in the mirror,
suggesting you take the toothbrushes elsewhere.
He's manipulating my desk,
gnawing at stacked envelopes,
ripping down Post-It-Notes®,
confiscating yellow markers.
He's dragging away the blue cartridge pens
and gray legal pads upon which all my
rough drafts of poems are written
and...

ACKNOWLEDGMENTS

The following poems are previously published. To those publications and their editors I extend my heartfelt thanks.

" A Concert Tuxedo", Peninsula Poets Anthology,
Poetry Society of Michigan (1995)

"Breakfast", Feathers, Fins & Fur Anthology,
Outrider Press (Illinois, 1999)

"Caribbean Discovery/British Virgin Islands"
Poetic Page (Michigan, 1997)

"Cat Sabbatical", Mutant Mule Review
(Ohio, 2000)

"Chicago Nights", 256 Shades of Grey Anthology,
(Wisconsin, 1996)

"Claysburg", Open Windows Anthology,
Golden Apple Press (Illinois, 1996)

"Crayola® Closet", Greater Flint Arts Council,
(Michigan, 1994)
Art/Life Limited Editions (California,1994)
Wordplay Magazine (Maine, 1996)

"Crystal Respite", Writers Exchange
(South Carolina, 1995)

"Dancing Advent", Quincy Writers Guild,
(Illinois, 1994)

"Evening Palette", Wings Magazine
(New Jersey, 1995)
Art/Life Limited Editions (California, 1996)
Freedoms' Just Another Word Anthology,
Outrider Press (Illinois, 1998)
Purple Patches Anthology,
(Pennsylvania, 1999)

"Fingered Night", Poetic Page (Michigan, 1996)

"Grand Island/North Light", The Beacon
(Michigan, 1995)

"Human Drought", Lucidity (Arkansas, 1996)

"January Effect", Poetic Page (Michigan, 1996)
Surprise Me (Oklahoma, 1996)

"John and Blanche", Remembrance
(South Carolina, 1996)

"Lake Superior Performance", The Pen
(Virginia, 1994)

"Latex White", Excursus Literary Arts Journal
(New York, 1995/96)
Art/Life Limited Editions
(California, 1996)
Zuzu's Petals Quarterly
(Pennsylvania, 1998)

"Mabel", Zuzu's Petals Quarterly
(Pennsylvania, 1996)

"Morning Green", Red Owl Magazine
     (New Hampshire, 1996)
     Earth Beneath, Sky Beyond Anthology,
     Outrider Press (Illinois, 2000)

"Playful", A Kiss Is Still A Kiss Anthology,
     Outrider Press (Illinois, 2001)

"Poetry Buffet", Rockford Art Museum,
     (Illinois, 1994)
     Virtute Et Morte (Pennsylvania, 1995)

"Primary Moves", Red Owl Magazine
     (New Hampshire, 1996)
     Verbal Expression (Michigan, 1996)

"Reception", Black River Syllabary
     (Michigan, 1995)

"Sour Milk", El Loco Foco, Chapultepec Press
     (Texas, 1996)
     Breakfast All Day (France, 1996)

"The Dog From Three Blocks Over", Paws & Tales,
     GDI Publishing (Massachusetts, 1998)
     Feathers, Fins & Fur Anthology,
     Outrider Press (Illinois, 1999)

"The Wait", Prairie Hearts Anthology,
     Outrider Press (Illinois, 1996)

"Wearing Pearls", Michigan Womens Times
     (Michigan, 1995)